THE SATIRICAL WORLD OF
JOSE PEREZ

TEXT BY
WAYMAN R. SPENCE, M.D.

FROM THE SATIRICAL WORLD ART MUSEUM
ESTES PARK, COLORADO

WRS
PUBLISHING

A Division of WRS Group, Inc.
Waco, Texas

First published in the United States of America in 1996
by WRS Publishing, A Division of WRS Group, Inc.,
701 N. New Road, Waco, Texas 76710.
Book design by Kenneth Turbeville.
Jacket design by Joe James.

Printed in Hong Kong

10 9 8 7 6 5 4 3 2 1

Library of Congress Cataloging-in-Publication Data

Spence, Wayman.
    The satirical world of Jose Perez / text by Wayman R. Spence.
        p.   cm.
    "From the satirical world of Jose Perez Art Museum, Estes Park, Colorodo."
    ISBN 1-56796-146-0
    1. United States--Politics and government--1989--Caricatures and
cartoons. 2. Medicine in art. 3. Medicine--Caricatures and cartoons.
4. Sports--Caricatures and cartoons. 5. American wit and humor, Pictorial.
I. Perez, José S., 1929–   . II. Title.
E839.5.S65
973.929'0207--dc20   96-6016
                                                              CIP

DEDICATION

America is a complex nation. Attempting to understand it can be frustrating. How is it possible that Republicans and Democrats constantly disagree on all issues? It is amazing how they can dispute and debate publicly and keep from laughing at each other. Politicians, however, can be an inspiration for historians, who keep records of man's behavior. They also are targets of the public's scorn, and they frequently provide materials for comedians and satirical artists, like me.

I therefore dedicate this book to Republicans and Democrats alike. A great many of them are good people. Under great pressure they struggle to keep this country of ours together. The book is also dedicated to those concerned with preserving our health and saving the environment, to those protecting both taxpayers and the poor, and to everyone with a sense of humor, who possess that God-given gift "to see ourselves as others see us."

ACKNOWLEDGMENTS

I thank Dr. Wayman Spence, who conceived the idea for this series of paintings and drawings and who wrote the introduction and descriptions for the paintings in this book. I also thank Pam Schreiber and Thomas Spence for their editing assistance and Kenneth Turbeville for his invaluable design work.

Jose Perez
December 14, 1995

Table of Contents

Introduction.. 4

The Man Behind The Art................................... 5

The President of the United States
of America 8

The Congress 10

The Department of Agriculture 12

The Department of Commerce.................... 14

The Department of Defense 16

The Department of Energy 18

The Department of Education................... 20

The Department of Housing &
Urban Development........................... 22

The Department of Health &
Human Services 24

The Department of the Interior 26

The Department of Justice 28

The Department of Labor 30

Post Office Department 32

The Department of Transportation........ 34

The Department of Treasury.................... 36

The Department of State............................. 38

The Department of Veterans Affairs 40

The Bureau of The Census 42

The Federal Bureau of Investigation 44

The Bureau of Indian Affairs 46

The Social Security Administration...... 48

The Supreme Court..................................... 50

A Day In Court 52

A Day In The Hospital.............................. 54

The Bureaucrats of Healthcare................ 56

The Coroner 58

The Emergency Room.................................. 60

The Family Practitioner 62

The Orthopedist 64

The Psychiatrist 66

The Surgeon 68

The Veterinarian 70

Baseball 72

Basketball 74

Boxing... 76

Football 78

Golf 80

Running 82

Skiing 84

Tennis 86

Weight Lifting 88

THE PRESIDENT — PEREZ

INTRODUCTION

There is little doubt that the American public is confused, frustrated and fed up with the antics of bureaucrats and so-called professionals. Daily stories of indefensible waste and fraud pour from our media to the point of such overload that we are inclined to either give up or throw the rascals out—or both. But just when it seems we can never find the right voice for our feelings, along comes Jose Perez. With the skills of a great artist and the candor of a common man, he exposes incompetence and greed in a unique way.

While today's political correctness may be the antithesis of artistic integrity, Jose Perez's art, in a most politically incorrect way, reminds us that something is fundamentally wrong in Washington. Our federal government is not only expensive, arcane, irrational and self-serving, but equally self-perpetuating. This strange system spawns thousands of projects every year upon which it spends trillions.

Perez's art illustrates how the vast majority of our government spending is dictated by the needs of special interest groups—bankers, lawyers, doctors, hospitals, corporations, farmers, universities, real estate brokers, social scientists, unions, ranchers, utilities, foreign interests, teachers, scientists, insurance companies, defense contractors, foundations, oil and gas firms, professional sports and countless others. He tells us that catastrophic incompetence is crippling the government's ability to serve all of our citizens. His paintings reveal the false concepts, bad management and empty promises that shape today's government, and help us reach the inevitable conclusion that Washington has gone fiscally mad.

All his life Jose Perez has indulged himself in a world of metaphor and paradox, through his wildly whimsical art. His black-and-white sketches—with their spontaneous, skittery style, reveal much about his soul. Fun to look at, and just as much fun to analyze, they are the first steps as he begins to think with his pencil about paintings to come, and leap wildly about from satire to near absurdity.

Perez has an uncanny ability to cause a flow of childhood emotions in all of us. He gathers his subject matter from industrial sites, crowds, parades, studies of history and regular visits to the zoo where he sketches the animals with the determined practice of a basketball player shooting thousands of baskets over and over in the gym.

At first glance we might think that Perez always has some deep symbolism in mind, with his rhinoceroses, elephants, centaurs, dogs, chimpanzees and assorted fowl, but a closer look shows that these are only a few elementary parts of his drawings and paintings. In general, his use of animals, babies and children, innocent and open minded, are his way of telling the viewer to step back and look at the world from a simpler view. His animal equations are humorous, but on a deeper level they arouse a feeling of dismay and disbelief at what we are doing to ourselves and the universe.

Perez's trademark is to catch the poetry of medieval times and the modern machine world, the body language of the haves and the have-nots, and the unspoken languages of the animal kingdom. His jibes draw praises from art critics and unsophisticated laymen alike, because he captures the disillusionment that is such a strong undercurrent in America today. As he deftly pricks our bubbles, he sometimes shocks our perceptions but never is really cruel. Perez, above all, is a kind and gentle person—but nobody's fool.

Called "the Will Rogers of American art," Perez has been internationally acclaimed for his socially-relevant paintings and drawings. In the long tradition of European visionary fantasy, exemplified by Hieronymus Bosch, the elder Brueghel, Goya, Kley, Cruikshank, Rowlandson and Daumier, his work promises to be remembered as the most outstanding American political satire, in the style of the old masters, this century. As The Wellcome Institute for the History of Medicine of London has said, "Perez is a genius. His work will be of historical interest."

Wayman R. Spence, M.D.,
Curator
The Satirical World of Jose Perez Art Museum
Estes Park, Colorado

THE MAN BEHIND THE ART

With a personality as unique as his art, Jose Perez has painted his way through life. His paintings are his voice, his method of expressing himself, his commentary on society.

Born in Houston, Texas, on June 30, 1929, of Mexican parents, Perez moved with his family to Mexico when he was five years old. Returning to the United States as a teenager, Perez swam across the border carrying his papers which proved he was a U.S. citizen. His brother, also a U.S. citizen, had lost his papers and so talked Jose into swimming back to their country. This incident is a foreshadowing of the personality Perez was to become.

Jose developed a sense of humor in his early years, and it's been an integral part of his life and his art ever since. Through years of working in menial jobs, through his struggle for recognition as an artist, through a bout with glaucoma—through all the trying times of his life, Jose Perez has maintained his sense of humor.

His career has evolved rather than developed. While Perez was working as a busboy, Mrs. Ruth Ford Van Dyke, owner and director of the Chicago Academy, noticed the drawings he had done on the backs of discarded menus. Mrs. Van Dyke invited Perez to study art at the academy and, within a few months, under the guidance of Louis Grell, a noted muralist, Perez was given a scholarship. He also studied with Allen St. John and William Mosby at the American Academy in Chicago.

Various events have interrupted his pursuit of art as a profession. In 1951, Perez was drafted into the army. After serving two years, he returned to the American Academy and studied art for another two years. He spent the next few years drifting from place to place, working at odd jobs—as a strawberry picker in Oregon, a construction worker in Houston, and a factory handyman in Chicago. Then, in 1958, he wandered to Washington, D.C., where he found the art ambience stimulating and where he started to paint professionally. His first art commission was to paint a series of large paintings depicting the American Revolution for the Drummer Boy Museum in Cape Cod, Massachusetts.

The confusion Perez had felt in earlier years evaporated when he began to concentrate on satirical art and pursue his profession seriously. His work is owned by a wide variety of art collectors in the United States and Europe, and in 1981, Houston, Texas declared a Jose S. Perez Day for its distinguished native artist.

In 1994, an exhibit at The National Library of Medicine of 28 Perez paintings on medicine was said to have received more attention than any other art exhibit in the library's history. CNN Television featured the exhibit worldwide, and selected Perez paintings are on tour to universities and museums. In 1996, a permanent collection of over 200 Perez paintings and drawings opened in Estes Park, Colorado, in The Satirical World of Jose Perez Art Museum.

Perez says of his own work: "Satirical painting suits my needs as an artist. It gives me the freedom to distort and yet remain in the spectrum of the fine arts. It is also my best way to communicate with my fellow man. The social comment, in which satirical art expresses its power, is without malice; it merely represents my personal view of the world as I see it, either from a historical point, the present, or the future."

THE PRESIDENT OF THE UNITED STATES OF AMERICA

While the public's image of the President of the United States of America—with his regal trappings, elegant mansion, Oval Office, Air Force One and "Hail to The Chief"—conjures up a sense of power, Perez's painting tells us that no one, but no one, is in charge in the nation's capital.

The President sits at the feet of the "father of our country," his head covered with a paper bag like a sports fan ashamed of his losing team. His body language bespeaks utter hopelessness. The muses of Greek mythology, shown as African-American, Hispanic, Asian and Caucasian, dance to a politically correct tune while the Klansman's eyes show the look of a frightened, fear-biting dog. The Statue of Liberty weeps as the immigrants stand at her feet. The Native American next to the flag-waving patriot seems to be blowing smoke at the President, while an assortment of contemporary weirdos, including a neo-Nazi and special interest groups, are all trying to get the attention of George Washington, or at least get a peek at what he is reading. Note particularly the punk protestor on the right whose sign proclaims that all men are created equal, but whose very presence proves that, if nothing else, they certainly don't mature equally.

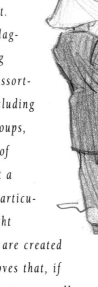

The President of the United States of America – 24" x 30" (61.5cm x 77cm)

THE CONGRESS

Whether on the Senate side or the House side, the Capitol Building reverberates with a never-ending parade of political celebrations and wakes. Elaborate dinners, beautiful chambers, spacious suites, and fleets of limousines are all part of the Capitol's everyday affairs, thanks to the taxpayers. And at no time are the parties bigger, the wine more plentiful and the girls friendlier than when there is a changing of the guard and a new majority party makes the old one a minority. In this painting, the Republicans are shedding their inhibitions and celebrating their victories as they waltz into power, while the Democrats back off from center stage, knowing their turn will come again.

The Congress – 24" x 30" (61.5cm x 77cm)

THE DEPARTMENT OF AGRICULTURE

*T*he Department of Agriculture is a cornucopia of waste without peer. Parkinson's law comes to life in this painting where farm programs have replaced ships in this prophetic equation on the strange behavior of government bureaucracies. If past trends continue, in another fifty years we will have only 150,000 full-time farmers, while the Department of Agriculture workers will have reached that same level.

Note the tuxedo-clad bureaucrat conductor bodaciously leading the lone farmer playing his "saxophone of plenty." The animals show more polite attention to the farmer's performance than the paid audience in the balcony. The inconspicuous sign reading "Plow For Sale" tucked in with the inebriated, celebratory bureaucrats tells the tale of the financial problems of today's farmers.

The Department of Agriculture – 24" x 30" (61.5cm x 77cm)

THE DEPARTMENT OF OMMERCE

*T*he subject of this painting is not immediately apparent to many viewers, but as soon as they see its title it all becomes clear. What better metaphor could there be for the U.S. Department of Commerce than a giant garage sale by Uncle Sam?

Perez remembers President Calvin Coolidge having said, "The business of America is business." This describes the main purpose of the Department of Commerce, to serve the businesspeople of the country. The department promotes foreign and domestic commerce, aids international corporations and small business enterprises, and develops uniform standards for all business products. Whether these functions do more harm than good is very debatable to most businesses.

The Department of Commerce – 24" x 30" (61.5cm x 77cm)

THE DEPARTMENT OF EFENSE

The purpose of this painting is not to offend the image of those who served in our Armed Forces so gallantly. Instead, Perez is pointing out the never-ending extremes to which mankind will go in improving its weapons of destruction, an endeavor which has been glorified since the invention of the sling.

In this mythical painting, an imaginary instrument of war, the Super-04, is about to be tested. This witless apparatus, capable of throwing a rock all of fifty feet, may look good to the gladiators, but has the population scared. The natives, stirred by the news, angrily band together to protest against the experiments, which they think may cause the end of the world. But it has always been the policy of those in power never to pay much heed to anyone who does not agree with their politics. Perez tells us that these characters will continue tinkering with their dangerous weapons until they finally invent a bomb so mighty that it will explode and cover the earth. When that happens, from within that cloud Perez hears a grating voice crying: "Hark, hark. Alone, I am alone. O Almighty, I am alone at last!"

The Department of Defense – 24" x 30" (61.5cm x 77cm)

THE DEPARTMENT OF ENERGY

The Department of Energy doesn't pay our electricity, gas or oil bills, and provides energy inexpensively to only a handful of Americans. For example, multibillion dollar notes for dams are paid equally by taxpayers, but only six percent of the nation receives cheaper electricity in return. Right now the five federal "power administrations" still owe the treasury over $12 billion, which they pay back at an interest rate less than half the rate at which the government borrows money – a giant yearly loss for taxpayers.

Like Socrates, U.S. taxpayers have to pay the Department of Energy for their own poison. Perez gets this point across as he shows the bureaucrats in Washington wining and dining while our land and air are being polluted, desecrated and destroyed. Only the birds seem to sense the gravity of the situation, as they look upon the scene and wonder what in the world mankind is up to.

The Department of Energy – 24" x 30" (61.5cm x 77cm)

THE DEPARTMENT OF DUCATION

*T*he Department of Education doesn't teach a single child and contributes only about five percent of the total cost of local education. Yet, it has its crosshairs trained on every school from New York City to Muskogee, Oklahoma.

While the Washington bureaucrats dream up new regulations restricting the very heart of American culture and the traditions upon which that culture was founded, the innocent little schoolchildren in this painting are ready to enter the classroom with their beautiful young teacher who would remind one of Shirley Jones' character, Marian, in "The Music Man." Behind the school door lurks the results of Washington's preoccupation with the politically correct but misguided substitution of unearned self-esteem rewards for reading, writing, arithmetic and old-fashioned family values. A knife and syringe are stuck in the door, condoms lie on the floor, gay and ethnic studies have replaced traditional history, and Judeo-Christian values have been distorted and impugned beyond recognition. Just who the hulking female figure peering over the door represents is not readily apparent, but then Perez often doesn't reveal everything he is thinking in his paintings.

The Department of Education – 24" x 30" (61.5cm x 77cm)

THE DEPARTMENT OF HOUSING & URBAN DEVELOPMENT

The Department of Housing & Urban Development was created in 1965 to deal with the housing problems of cities. In spite of its rock-solid name, it was formed by a combination of several government agencies and is hardly known for its cost-containing accountability.

As with most Washington pork-barrel factories, everything at HUD begins with a committee. These committees have enormous power in setting up appropriations that include all sorts of little gifts for the folks at home—a subsidized housing complex, a university building, a road, a gymnasium, a grant or whatever. The fact that it may be neither legal nor ethical for taxpayers' money to be given away to private institutions with no federal function never seems to phase the bureaucrats of HUD.

The Department of Housing & Urban Development – 24" x 30" (61.5cm x 77cm)

THE DEPARTMENT OF  HEALTH & HUMAN SERVICES

"*D*uplication and Overlap" is not the name of a Washington law firm, but the theme song of America's federally controlled social services. Yet in spite of the system's good intentions, not uncommonly the very people who need help the most are overlooked. Like the vast majority of America's caregivers, the towering figure of the Department of Health & Human Services means well but simply can't cope with all the people's problems. Thousands of human research grants haven't solved anything. Unless some sort of realistic self-help mentality miraculously descends upon the population, the future will in all likelihood become even more grim.

The Department of Health & Human Services – 24" x 30" (61.5cm x 77cm)

THE DEPARTMENT OF THE INTERIOR

As the nation's principal conservation agency, the
Department of the Interior is responsible for most of our
federally-owned public lands and natural resources. This includes
fostering the wisest use of our land and water, protecting our fish
and wildlife, and preserving the environmental and cultural
values of our national parks and historic sites. The department
also assesses our mineral resources and works to assure that
their development is in the best interest
of all the people.

Perez takes no prisoners as he
satirically shows the bureaucrats
wining and dining on roast buffalo.
The pristine mountain scene on the
wall shows how the department tries to
portray their care of our land. Reality,
however, is shown in the chaotic
destruction going on behind their
backs. One doesn't have to be an
environmental activist to see
through their pomposity. Just count
the number of ways the land, air
and wildlife are abused in this
disturbingly insightful painting.

The Department of the Interior – 24" x 30" (61.5cm x 77cm)

The Department of ustice

A hundred years ago, there were 1,500 employees in the Department of Justice. Today, the department has a budget of over $12 billion and 100,000 employees, all supervised by an Attorney General appointed by the President.

In addition to maintaining law and order through the Supreme Court, circuit courts of appeal, district courts, courts of claims, courts of customs and patent appeals, territorial courts, the Federal Bureau of Investigation and the federal prison system, the Department of Justice handles lawsuits for the U. S. government.

In this painting, a citizen is being weighed on the scales of justice. The government's attorney is represented as the court jester showing his card tricks. The haughty federal judge, with the security of a lifetime appointment, demonstrates little interest in the case. Not surprisingly, Justice, hiding behind his large figure, hangs her head in despair as the trial goes on. The vultures waiting for the decision are symbolic of Washington's media, and a TV camera records it all for the nightly news. The citizens seated about the table read their newspapers and discuss the case, while stewn about the floor are pages from TV, book and movie contracts.

The Department of Justice – 24" x 30" (61.5cm x 77cm)

The Department of ABOR

None of Perez's political paintings are more troubling than this parable of the labor movement as it watches its factories and jobs leaving for foreign lands. The draft horses are a metaphor of labor's roots in the industrial revolution, and remind us of the struggles between workers and employers throughout the last two centuries. Who has been right and who has been wrong? Where have all labor's heroes gone, and what about its scoundrels? What would management have done without labor? What will labor do when its jobs are all gone? No wonder Perez's labor board seems at such a loss as it watches the Pete Moose & Co. moving wagon led by the pied piper of management.

PEREZ ON THE

30

The Department of Labor – 24" x 30" (61.5cm x 77cm)

POST OFFICE DEPARTMENT

No mere painting can cover the inefficiences of the U.S. Postal Service—that would require volumes. Perez indulges in a bit of nostalgia as he shows Father Time remembering back to the 1940s when people received two mail deliveries a day, stamps cost 3¢ and postmen braved "snow, rain, heat and gloom of night for swift completion of their appointed rounds." There were also no acts of random violence in our post offices, and attorneys didn't sue for millions when dogs bit postmen.

Maybe it used to be the postmen who braved the snow, rain, heat and darkness to deliver the mail, but today it is more apt to be the customers because over one fourth of all postal offices are too small to deliver mail. "We could easily save $150 million a year by closing these small offices down," a government auditor has said.

*P*ost *O*ffice *D*epartment – 24" x 30" (61.5cm x 77cm)

THE DEPARTMENT OF TRANSPORTATION

*F*ormed in 1966 as the twelfth department of government, the Department of Transportation is charged with administering and controlling all forms of transportation, including air traffic and the Coast Guard. How are they doing? Ask Perez!

Although the subject is serious, this painting is hilariously funny to look at. Old biplanes dodge jets and UFOs, helicopters hop around like dragonflies, and trains, cars, trucks and boats are heaped up in one huge pile. The fly-swatting bureaucrat perched atop all this mess represents the government's disjointed attempts to introduce order into chaos. All in all, it reminds one of a combination of the worst of LA freeways, getting a cab on a rainy afternoon in New York and Christmas Eve at Chicago's O'Hare Airport. The distraught eagle tells us that, as always, our fine feathered friends come out second best when special interest groups control any part of our environment.

The Department of Transportation – 24" x 30" (61.5cm x 77cm)

THE DEPARTMENT OF TREASURY

Nothing attracts a crowd more than a free handout. In this case, the goose is turning out money for everyone, with no golden eggs to back up the currency. But until inflation catches up with this scheme, the crowd won't know the difference.

A multitude of lobbyists, obviously all after money, are mixed in with the crowd of the needy and the greedy. While the well-dressed lobbyists are easy to spot, the needy and the greedy are not so easy to discern.

What alcohol, tobacco and firearms have to do with the Treasury Department has always been a mystery, but that's where these brave agents have wound up on the organizational chart of Washington. The machine-gun wielding NRA character plopped on the balcony tells his own story with his body language. The mountain brew flowing from the homemade still gets about as much attention in the painting as it does in real life.

The Department of Treasury – 24" x 30" (61.5cm x 77cm)

THE DEPARTMENT OF TATE

The chief duties of the Department of State are to maintain friendly relations between the U.S. and other countries, to build up foreign trade and commerce, and to protect U.S. citizens and their property abroad. The department aids in making and enforcing treaties, and through its ambassadors, ministers and consuls, works with foreign governments.

This painting depicts a reception to which high level representatives from all over the world have been invited. While most guests are properly dressed, a couple of less savory visitors have slipped into the back of the room, unnoticed by security. None of the other guests appear to pay any particular attention to them or their weapons, as their attention is focused on the President, who is either bored or confused by the whole gathering. The woman at the far right with a child on her back is the only apparent representative of the third world, which, of course, has considerably more than a third of the world's population.

The Department of State – 24" x 30" (61.5cm x 77cm)

THE DEPARTMENT OF ETERANS AFFAIRS

*O*f all the Perez paintings on politics, this is the only one without even a touch of humor. Perez feels that there is no subject more serious than war, and it shows in this poignant scene of a mythical American soldier coming home to the reality of loneliness and despair.

The flag hangs limp, the landscape is barren, the sky is gray and no life is seen on the horizon; all a metaphor of the cruel letdown so many veterans experience after risking their lives for their country. Government, represented by the Capitol on the distant horizon, seems very far away to this lonely returning soldier. His bare waist, slumped shoulders and downcast shadow speak for themselves.

The Department of Veterans Affairs – 24" x 30" (61.5cm x 77cm)

THE BUREAU OF THE CENSUS

In 1789, the Founding Fathers provided in article 1, section 2, clause 3 of the Constitution that the "actual enumeration of citizens shall be made within three years after the first meeting of Congress, and every subsequent ten years in a manner as they shall by law direct." Today, this giant polling operation spends over $300 million a year, and our next census will cost taxpayers about $4 billion dollars.

The Census Bureau is a perfect model of Washington waste. Not only do the census probers ask name and address, but sex, race, income, property, household furnishings and dozens of other impertinent questions. And if we don't answer correctly they even threaten federal prosecution. No wonder the characters in Perez's painting show little interest or friendliness as the gigantic census taker walks through their midst. Head-counting may be part of our Constitution, but an invasion of privacy is not.

The Bureau of the Census – 24" x 30" (61.5cm x 77cm)

THE FEDERAL BUREAU OF INVESTIGATION

The stereotypical, trench-coated FBI agent stands in the middle of the table almost invisible as he tries like a Boy Scout in a den of thieves to get some attention and respect. Meanwhile, the rogues of society, representing gangs, organized crime, and plain old crooks, are planning an all-out attack like pirates of old. This would all seem like great fun if it weren't for the cold reality of today's daily headlines of guerrilla warfare, maniacal killings and drug and gun trafficking, for which the real FBI is just about as effective a deterrent as the agent in this painting.

The Federal Bureau of Investigation – 24" x 30" (61.5cm x 77cm)

THE BUREAU OF NDIAN AFFAIRS

*T*he Bureau of Indian Affairs is the federal agency with primary responsibility for working with Indian tribal governments and Alaskan native village communities. Today there are over one million Native Americans living on or near hundreds of Indian reservations, and approximately the same number scattered throughout the land.

While no one in Washington is satisfied with the state of Indian affairs, no one seems to know what to do about it, except to throw more money at the problem each successive year. "The Great White Father" spends over $5 billion each year for Indians, many of whom still live in near abject poverty with an unemployment rate close to 50%.

Perez's painting, in which the bureaucrat rides double with the Indian as they survey the sprawling landscape of western civilization, tells us that if there is a possible answer to the Washington-Indian dilemma, it lies in the fact that our bureaucrats should leave the Indian alone and give more power to the tribes. They could hardly do worse than Washington's waste and mismanagement, and besides, we owe them something better.

The Bureau of Indian Affairs – 24" x 30" (61.5cm x 77cm)

THE **S**OCIAL SECURITY ADMINISTRATION

In spite of the fact that medium-income Americans now pay more in FICA taxes than they do in straight income taxes, by the year 2020 there simply won't be enough money in the kitty to handle the baby boomers, who will be starting to retire in enormous numbers. But when all the money's gone, it won't be the fault of recipients of Social Security benefits. The guilt will belong to the politicians, who spent the surplus FICA money on everything but the aged, or the future aged.

In this Perez scene, Washington's bureaucrats are meeting to handle the Social Security crisis. The great scheme founded by FDR in the Old Age and Survivors Insurance Act of 1935 is going belly up, or more aptly put, future-broke. Just as threatening to the hearts of politicians is the fear that the public will figure out that the reason for the system's demise is that the government has been borrowing (stealing) hundreds of billions of dollars from their Social Security system for its own general fund, with no hopes of paying it back.

The Social Security Administration – 24" x 30" (61.5cm x 77cm)

THE UPREME COURT

Nine people with lifetime appointments, out of a population of 250 million, vote 5-4 and the entire course of our country changes, until the next vote, which may go 4-5 the other way. No wonder Justice herself seems so sarcastically resigned as she perches atop the shoulders of the stoic Chief Justice of the U.S. Supreme Court.

The judges of Perez's Supreme Court are gigantic and positioned to tower above the small bodies of the little people. Nevertheless, the crowd of diminutive characters has succeeded in at least getting the attention of the robed justices. Of course, one gets the impression that the dignified group really won't pay too much attention to the masses as they make decisions that the Founding Fathers never dreamed would be delegated to nine old men and women.

The Supreme Court – 24" x 30" (61.5cm x 77cm)

DAY IN COURT

*A*ll the fears, angers and frustrations of our nation's chaotic political system are exemplified by just one day in any court of law in our land. Perez painted "A Day in Court" after having spent a day in court himself over a minor legal dispute. The parables and metaphors of his insight are visible in every part of this canvas. The whole scene comes together in the helpless look on the face of the judge, who bears an unmistakable resemblance to Perez himself.

One can look at this large painting for weeks and still discover fresh messages and new characters previously unnoticed. Describing this painting is like describing a parade, so many of the personalities seem the same, and yet they're all different. From white power to black power, to gay power, to taxpayer's power, as the sign held by the robed fellow next to the long-haired dog in the lower left corner says, maybe "THE END **IS** NEAR."

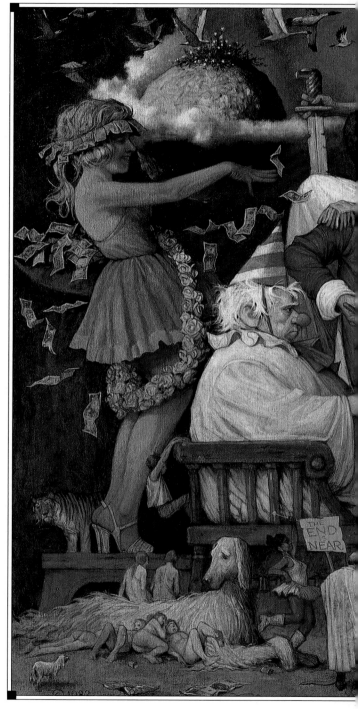

A *D*ay in *C*ourt – *48" x 96" (123cm x 246cm)*

DAY IN THE HOSPITAL

This masterfully complex painting sets the stage for Perez' series on medicine. It is not just a story about doctors, because Perez does not treat medicine as the exclusive turf of doctors. Rather, it shows the inescapable relationships between healers, sufferers, disease, and death. The conglomerate that brings these components together is what we call our health-care system. In reality, it should be called our illness-care system. This painting holds up a mirror to the very essence of the system—our hospitals.

After focusing on the large, central doctor, one's eye is tempted to move in all directions to scenes and sub-scenes throughout the canvas. But, if you will, first look at the doctor's facial expression and body language. This very human figure seems to be wondering what in the world he should do with all the suffering humanity he confronts.

The patient on the operating table—who looks as if he's just about to expire—is getting a lot of attention from the medical staff. Merlin the Magician is positioned next to the patient, perhaps to help him cross the River Styx. Is all this care too late? Would it be wiser to free up the doctors to help patients with better chances of survival?

The priest-like fellow in the purple robe holds a burning candle, perhaps trying to shed light on the situation, or maybe suggesting that modern medicine is closer to that of past centuries than we like to think. One hundred years from now, will blood transfusions, scalpels, and radiation-scattering X-rays seem as primitive as bleeding and purging seem to us? Will the depersonalized treatment of patients—shown by the robot being oiled—result in robot-like people, who take no responsibility for their own care?

Animal rights activists will identify with the orangutan holding the placard, while the children below him remind us that children have rights, too, and not to be abused is one of those rights.

As the Grim Reaper in the lower right-hand corner comes to claim his prey, we realize that the wisdom of Solomon could not solve the needs of modern society with all its pressure groups, here shown by the demonstrators in the hall balcony. Perez himself is seen painting on a crumbling wall the words, "Les Misérables," an apt description of the patients in our system, and something of a double entendre: Perez' daughter spent two years traveling with the Broadway musical of that name.

A Day in the Hospital – 48" x 96" (123cm x 246cm)

THE BUREAUCRATS OF HEALTHCARE

Nothing Washington ever created has been more profitable or more damning for healthcare than Medicare. Because of an unholy alliance between government bureaucracy and private industry, it has been legal to sell five-dollar aspirins and ten-dollar diapers to sick, elderly people who don't even know what their government has done. This license to steal has made millionaires out of countless entrepreneurs over the last three decades.

Perez's whimsical, satirical genius comes through at its best in the centrally-placed, villainous puppeteer, a caricature of Dickens' Scrooge, impairing the doctor and manipulating the puppet patients. While the nurses are helplessly buried in paperwork, the bureaucrats in Washington are above it all and arrogantly toasting their own good health. The chap riding the paper airplane enjoys the scene, and is not the least bit bothered by the salvage yard of patients or the environmental destruction behind him. He must be one of those managed care providers, pragmatically capable of adjusting to the changing winds of medical economics.

56

The Bureaucrats of Healthcare – 24" x 30" (61.5cm x 77cm)

THE ORONER

The coroner usually has the last word in medicine, because he does the autopsy. He tells everyone else what the correct diagnosis should have been and why the treatments didn't work. He can also be the ace in the hole for a malpractice defense attorney, and the secret weapon of the plaintiff's attorney.

In this painting, the tables seem to have been turned on the coroner. Death has come back to tell the coroner what was done incorrectly. As Death straddles the Jungian snake amid a horde of rats on the morgue floor—symbolic of the carriers of the disease that caused the plagues of earlier times—he points an accusatory finger at the doctor and his assistants.

The assistants may know about many more mistakes, judging from their fears of the defiant skeleton. Even the witch doctor looks a little frazzled as he tries to use his magic to shift the blame to someone else.

Notice the autopsy knife, which the coroner has dropped on the floor in fright. What fresh mistakes have been made on the body on the morgue table? Is the coroner trying to bring this fellow back to life with all those strange contraptions? Is this what Death is chiding him about?

The Coroner – 24" x 30" (61.5cm x 77cm)

THE EMERGENCY ROOM

While planning this painting, Perez spent a night at a large city hospital emergency room and was reminded of the night he and his wife had taken his ill grandson to the ER. There, Perez and his wife found a long line of people waiting to be cared for, with nowhere else to go for treatment. Although most of the crowd waited patiently, one old man grew tired of waiting and decided to do something about it. He stretched himself out in the middle of the floor, pretending to be near death. Immediately, two men came with a stretcher, picked the old fellow up, and hauled him into an examining room.

In his painting, Perez has the members of the medical staff towering over the crowd of diminutive patients, symbolizing the sometimes intimidating nature of today's hospitals. While death waits in the form of a vulture perched atop the stoplight, the TV cameraman tries to catch a little drama for the eleven o'clock news.

The lame, the blind, the pregnant, and the sick migrate endlessly to the center of the canvas, where they are unceremoniously shoveled onto the examining table like pieces of coal into a furnace, with no privacy or sanctity.

While the antique ambulance is a reminder of the days of World War I, the contemporary posters on the wall bring today's health-education efforts into view. The policeman tries to stop the flow of patients. As the street vendor displays her wares, she views the scene and, like so many of us, is glad she is only a spectator—at least for today.

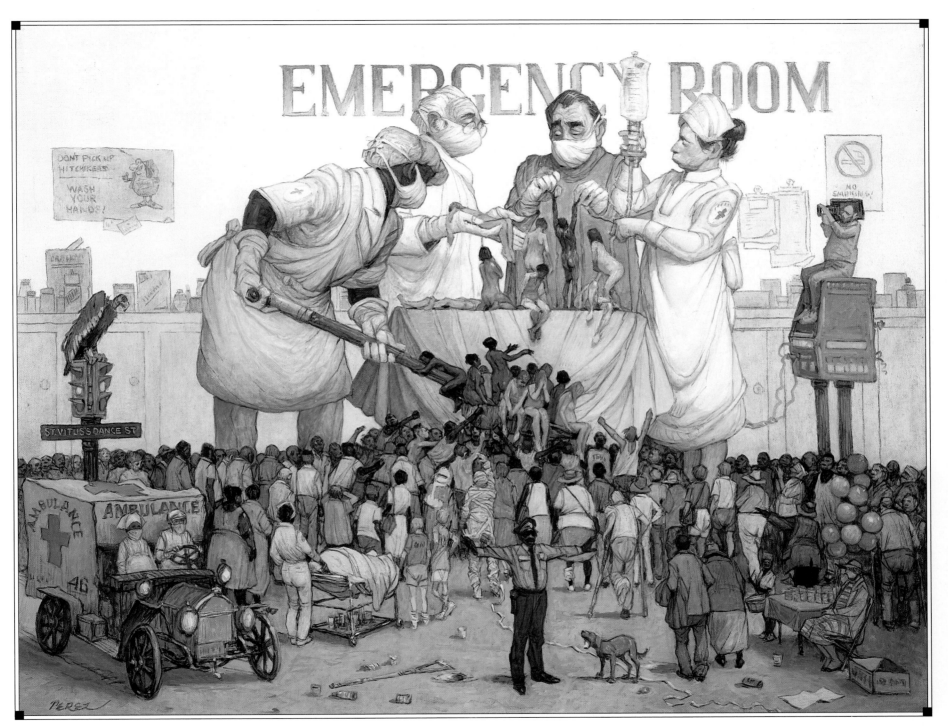

The Emergency Room – 24" x 30" (61.5cm x 77cm)

THE FAMILY PRACTITIONER

This painting reminds us that doctors are human, too. They get worn out and weary and succumb to the same stresses as their patients. This poor family "doc" is like the old woman who lived in a shoe. He has so many patients he doesn't know what to do.

Since the doctor appears to be overcome by the demands of his practice, his assistant patiently offers him some of his own medicine. Meanwhile, the patients appear to be faring better than the doctor.

The small, malnourished black child and the undernourished white child swinging on the rope are symbols of world hunger. The crying, naked child held by the mother in shorts, and the lady with the deaf old man tell us that most of us will be as children twice.

The man sitting on the doctor's knee nonchalantly reads the paper, exemplifying the ability of some people to remain detached, no matter what the impending diagnosis may be. The inebriated chap between the doctor's feet shows another way of coping with examining-room anxiety.

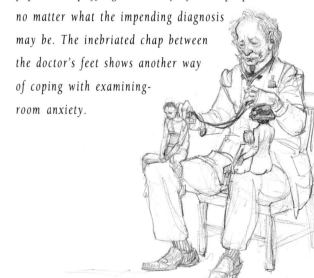

The Family Practitioner – 24" x 30" (61.5cm x 77cm)

THE ORTHOPEDIST

A gargantuan figure, the doctor in this painting sits on his unique throne of bones and conveys a sense of power and authority. The ruins of the Roman wall and the Egyptian nurse standing in front of the doctor are signs that orthopedics is one of the oldest branches of medicine. In fact, archaeologists and paleontologists have found evidence of set bones dating back to primitive times.

Various athletes approach the doctor's throne to ask in reverential fashion for healing of their sports injuries. They probably already know that complete obedience to the doctor's commands will be demanded of them. The doctor will surely tell them to stop doing whatever they are doing, or, if they're not doing something, to begin it.

The enormous size accorded the doctor could reflect the fact that many orthopedists played football in their college days and still enjoy being on the sidelines in their role as doctors. Or it could simply be acknowledgment of the degree of trust placed in him by his patients, who are probably the most compliant of patients because of their desire to return to their sport as soon as possible.

The Orthopedist – 24" x 30" (61.5cm x 77cm)

THE PSYCHIATRIST

This is the first painting Perez did for this collection, and it set the stage for the mind games he would play with each specialty. While a psychiatrist is supposed to be thinking about a patient's case, the psychiatrist in Perez' work is preoccupied with his own problems: His mistress is playing with his hair while illusions and delusions fill the room. Napoleon is there, with both arms shown in an uncharacteristic stance and a large Number One on his back. An anthropomorphic parrot awaits his turn to talk, a monkey is climbing on or off the doctor's back, an egg waits to hatch or be stepped on, and a dragon seems poised to strike. Trumpet sounds fill the air near the doctor's ear, and the drunken gladiator doesn't seem to know where to begin as he tells the doctor his troubles.

It's interesting to note the shoes on the psychiatrist. Is it significant that they are untied, or that they are running shoes?

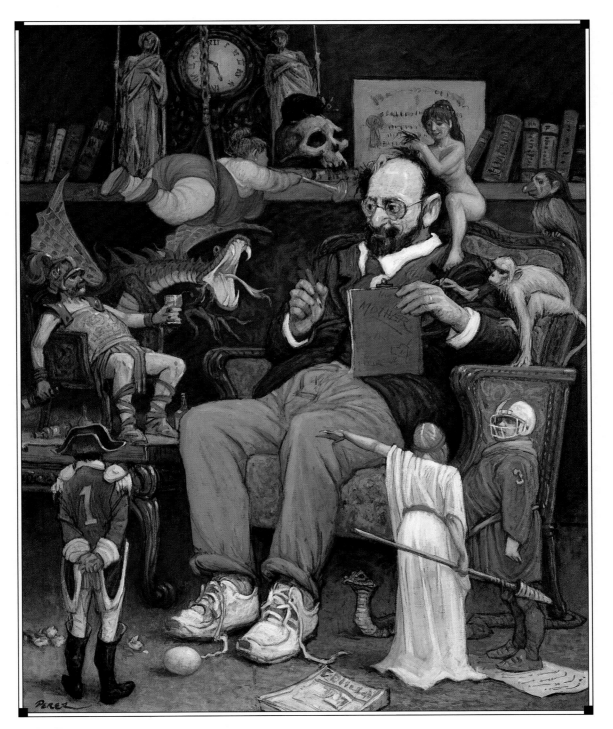

The Psychiatrist – 30" x 24" (77cm x 61.5cm)

THE URGEON

A**lthough** it may remind one of a repair shop, the operating room goes far beyond that. It represents the incredible innovations in medicine that have allowed man to repair and replace body parts. Someday we might be able to keep human beings running indefinitely, rather like restored antique cars.

Perez's block-and-tackle rig is testimony to the inestimable value of practical tools in even the most complicated of technical situations. It's somewhat reminiscent of one of those television scenes in which a white-coated doctor comes dashing out of a helicopter carrying a donor heart in a polystyrene drink cooler.

The size of the patient in relation to the size of the repairmen—the surgeons—is an interesting feature of this painting, perhaps to express the intricacy of the human body.

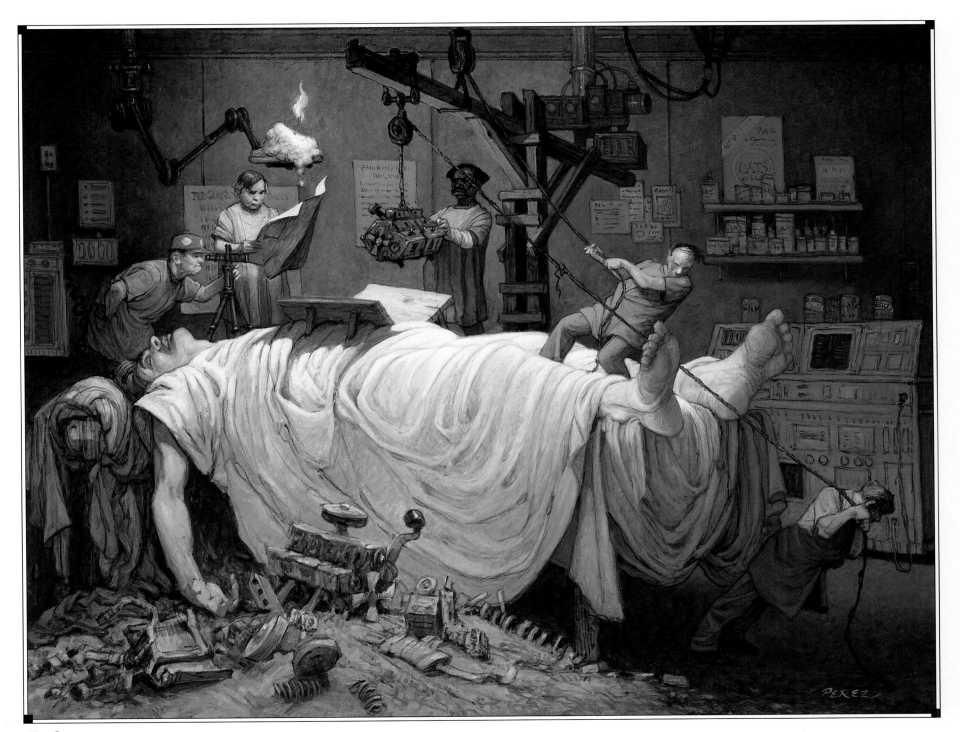

The Surgeon – 24" x 30" (61.5cm x 77cm)

THE VETERINARIAN

Perez has an unusual love for animals of all kinds, and it shows in this painting. His veterinarian has a kind and wise demeanor that would do justice to the veterinarian in **All Creatures Great and Small.**

With the baby orangutan clearly bawling out a high note as the doctor removes an offending splinter, the concerned creatures of the woods gather around to await the result with an empathy that perhaps only animals can show. Body language is certainly not limited to humans, and this work of art tells us that veterinary medicine has rewards that human medicine cannot share.

The Veterinarian – 24" x 30" (61.5cm x 77cm)

# BASEBALL

*J*ust as in the real game, there's no doubt who the star is in this painting. But from the looks of the hurler on the mound, who would ever guess that he's a multimillionaire with all the privileges of the rich and famous.

The cocky batter whose center of gravity leans perilously into the strike zone dares the pitcher to get a fastball by him. The plate ump hides behind the gorilla catcher, who plays with no protective gear and is obviously the toughest guy on the diamond.

How many photos can be taken of the moment of truth as ball meets bat? The answer seems to be — never enough. Meanwhile, in the stands behind home plate, there's no fear of foul tips, only relaxed enjoyment of the whole scene. Who would have thought when baseball was first played at Cooperstown in 1839, that it would become a worldwide sport, and an Olympic one at that?

The delightful little rabbits who almost steal the scene represent all the kids that used to watch minor league games in the good old days, through knotholes in the fences or by sneaking into the park under and over the boards.

Finally, guess what all those pockmarks are in the infield grass. They're probably spots where tobacco juice has rendered biological life impossible. I wonder what it's doing to the mouth of our pitcher?

*B*aseball – 24" x 30" (61.5cm x 77cm)

BASKETBALL

While most people think of basketball as a game of giants played in an endlessly long season on TV, the game owes its real soul to the millions of driveways, playgrounds and small-town gyms where regularly guys play.

Perez's mad rebound scramble looks a little like a rugby scrim, but the ball floating above the mass of outstretched arms lifts the eye upward, unlike the down and dirty direction of rugby.

Every time one examines this painting a new, interesting character seems to emerge. Notice the poor guy on the bottom of the pile with the ankle wrap all undone. The blasé kid sitting in front of number 0 is managing to stay cool no matter what, and number 28 shows that some white guys _can_ jump, although this player's vertical leap is probably about six inches.

Every player from the YMCA to the pros has all sorts of mixed emotions about spectators, whose personalities range from assassins to mothers. These Jekyll-and-Hyde vicarious participants in the game have become as important to television as the players themselves. Spike Lee and Jack Nicholson must be somewhere in this crowd.

Finally, the great Larry Bird would surely feel an affinity with the bird flying toward the ball. But what in the world is a nest doing in Perez's basket? Maybe he's just trying to say that these guys are such poor shots there's not much need to keep it clean.

Basketball – 24" x 30" (61.5cm x 77cm)

OXING

It's hard to figure out where the best fight is in this arena — in the ring or in the stands. The white-clad referee takes one's eye first to the ring where the bloodied and beaten fighter in the blue trunks is being declared the winner, while the poor loser in the red trunks, fresh and unscathed, dubiously accepts the judge's bewildering decision like so many other political losers in olympics past. And from the looks of things, the ring announcer had better get himself back into the safety of the ring, or those pugilistic fans gone crazy may kill him next.

The moral of this painting is to never leave your fate in the hands of judges susceptible to political influences — in the ring or out.

Boxing – 24" x 30" (61.5cm x 77cm)

FOOTBALL

American football certainly can be accused of being a violent game, and all the metaphors from bombs to blitzes support this allegation. But Perez says that football is first and foremost a big boy's way of playing king-of-the-mountain.

In this painting, the elephant backfield has done its work — the football has crossed the goal line and the medieval cheerleaders have begun their touchdown dance. The faceless fans in the stands can now cheer or groan, depending on which side they sit. How can anyone look at this playful scene and not imagine football in the Olympics?

The 1932 Summer Olympics in Los Angeles featured 1,328 athletes from 37 countries competing in 128 events. The 1996 Summer Games in Atlanta, Georgia will host approximately 11,000 athletes from 196 countries competing for medals in 271 events. There will be room for football. And when it happens, can you imagine what a USA dream team made up of future Joe Montanas and Jerry Rices will do to teams from Chile and Portugal? 400-0 might be a close game.

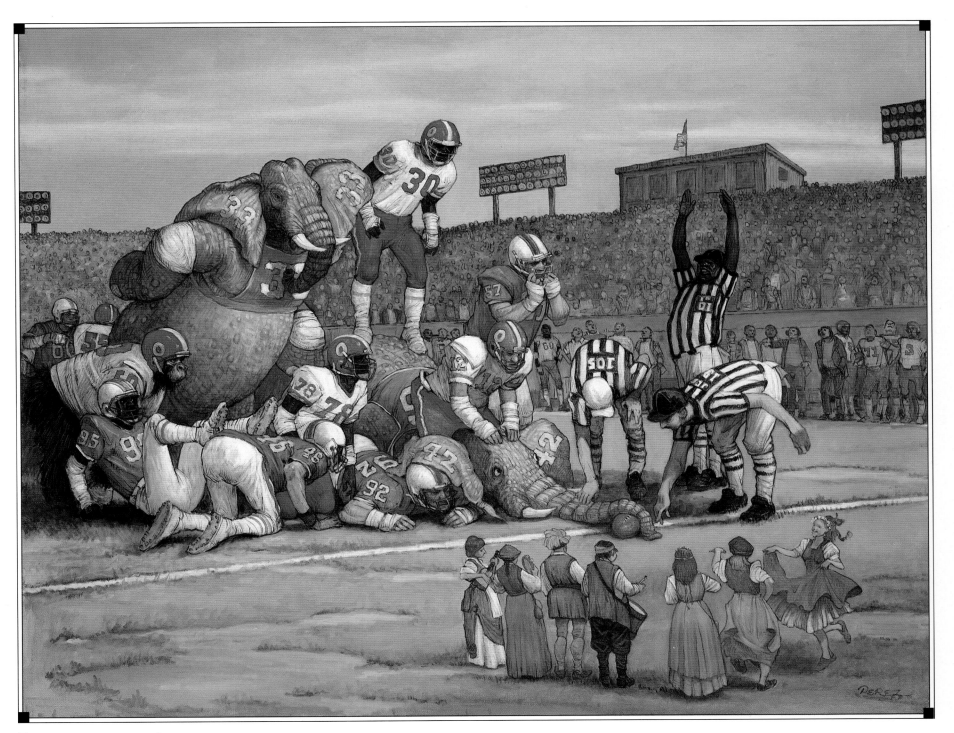

*F*ootball – 24" x 30" (61.5cm x 77cm)

GOLF

*T*his painting should charm the pants off of any golfer. Perez has depicted an unlikely accident: a golf ball has struck an innocent rabbit. In keeping with the spirit of our politically correct times, a protest is being staged by all the natural inhabitants of the golf course. As the elected spokesman reads the charges brought against the golfers, accusing them of violating animal rights, the body language of the golfers ranges from defiance to a little bit ashamed.

Perez is a great lover of animals, and suggests that golf courses should adopt different rules for different times. Golfers play during the day, and the critters use the course at night.

While golf is one of the few worldwide sports not yet credited with Olympic status, surely it will join the group. If boxing with all of its brutality and judging scandals, modern pentathlon which is neither modern nor telegenic, synchronized swimming which is little more than shipwreck ballet, and rhythmic gymnastics, where an inadvertent exposure of a bra strap means automatic point deduction, can be Olympic sports, then golf with all of its heritage, dignity and television appeal will certainly someday grace the events.

*G*olf – 24" x 30" *(61.5cm x 77cm)*

# RUNNING

*E*very character in this race deserves the eyes' undivided attention, but like a real race, one's tendency is to lose the personality of each runner in the mass of the pack.

The tortoise appears to be in the lead, and the court attendant's sign says they're about to begin the final lap. Has the poor tortoise been lapped, or is he really beating the hare again?

Who is the centaur carrying in his arms, and who is the poor, courageous fellow with the blue toga personifying as he tries to crawl his way to the finish line? Real marathoners have on occasion looked as fatigued.

Notice the racer in the football suit. He apparently can't wait to turn pro. What about the ostrich coming up on the left of the rhinoceros? It's anybody's guess who will win Perez's race.

The rabbits are naturally cheering for their own species, while the rest of the spectators seem pretty impartial, except for the two Greeks at the top left who may get rather nasty if their favorite doesn't win. All in all, this menagerie of spectators is amazingly like the cross section seen at any club road race.

Running – 24" x 30" (61.5cm x 77cm)

SKIING

*L*ook out! Here comes the overweight, out-of-shape, out-of-control, middle-aged flat lander who hits the slopes once a year and scares the mountain natives half to death. The two chaps standing side by side have seen it all before, and know there is no use in even trying to give this skier any advice because he won't listen anyway. At least three other skiers have gone down in his tracks, and the rabbit running for his life may or may not make it to safety. The penguins are unperturbed because they have enough sense to stay off the slopes when flat landers are on a skiing vacation.

Skiing – 24" x 30" (61.5cm x 77cm)

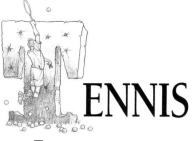

TENNIS

The real fun in watching tennis is at court side, where one can hear the bangs of the ball, feel the grunts from the players, and watch their between-point antics. Television may offer close-ups, but it loses the visceral parts of the game.

Because this is mixed doubles, there's no big crowd and no TV cameras. Like any typical club match, the males are trying to dominate and show their toughness. But the women control themselves and are not the least intimidated.

This scene is filled with numerous stereotypes from the bored, sleeping netsman to the military stances of the ball boys. The crowd has an international flavor and, unlike tennis crowds of years past, is openly enthusiastic as it enjoys cheering for its favorite. While the action on center court takes one's eye at first, the emotional scene is stolen by the little girl at the lemonade stand. Somehow one knows that she'll be a star herself someday.

Tennis – 30" x 24" (77cm x 61.5cm)

WEIGHT LIFTING

This wonderful painting defies a simple interpretation; it is perhaps the most psychoanalytical of any of Perez's sports art. One can study the work for hours and still discover a figure, expression or prop completely overlooked before.

Perez says ancient myths concerning Atlas holding up the world led him to this surrealistic expression of a weight lifter trying to military press a barbell weighted with elephants and rhinoceroses on one side and a group of people on the other. Notice the barbell is leaning to the human side, which outweighs even the largest of animals.

Study the expressions of the various spectators. They're not actually exaggerated at all. The real spectators at a weight-lifting competition are every bit as much fun to watch as the lifters themselves.

Perez's sense of anatomy is absolutely exquisite in his treatment of the lifter, from his red knees to his mammoth, arched posture. Perhaps if the lifter can pause long enough, with the barbell resting on his chest and shoulders, a few more human weights will fall off and he'll be able to hoist this preposterous weight above his head.

Weight Lifting – 24" x 30" (61.5cm x 77cm)